Small Arms
CHILDREN OF CONFLICT

Garrett – thanks.
for the great class
and your marvelous invention

Small Arms

CHILDREN OF CONFLICT

PHOTOGRAPHS BY MICHAEL KIENITZ

Small Arms
PRODUCTIONS

Book design and composition by Patrick JB Flynn
   (The Flynstitute, Madison, Wisconsin)

Duotones produced by Michael Kienitz

Text edited by Susan Day

This catalog was sponsored in part by the Chazen Museum of Art where an accompanying exhibition of the photographs was displayed September 8–October 28, 2007.

■ SMALL ARMS PRODUCTIONS
   Madison, Wisconsin, United States of America
   Internet: **www.michaelkienitz.com**
   Email: **photo4u@michaelkienitz.com**

To my wife,

*Dr. Beverly Kienitz, whose steadfast
encouragement and support made
this possible. And to all the children who
appear in these photographs for their courage
and mischief, and to the present generation
of children who, alas, are forced to deal
with continuing political and economic
conflict in their own creative ways.
And for my parents,
Bonnie and Jack.*

Cartographies of Impossible and Possible Worlds

BY PATRICIA R. ZIMMERMANN

Elsewhere Is Here

A languid, unraveling shoelace cascades over worn, dusty sneakers. The little boy, maybe five years old, wears a fitted camouflage uniform with crumpled epaulets, a brimmed military-style hat covering his head. He grips the arms of a scratched wooden chair with his small hands. His feet do not touch the floor. He looks intently to the side, half of his face shaded by the hat, the other half lit by the sunlight.

This photograph, by photojournalist Michael Kienitz, is titled *The Little General* (Peshawar, Pakistan, 1984). It is one of thirty-six images from *Small Arms—Children of Conflict*, a moving retrospective of three decades of Kienitz's photography. The exhibition maps how politically and economically driven conflict and violence envelop the bodies of children across the globe.

During the war in Vietnam, Kienitz was sitting in his political philosophy class at the University of Wisconsin in Madison. Outside, he could hear the screams and chants of the students involved in the antiwar movement. Later, he realized the local news media failed to accurately describe what he had witnessed—and heard—for himself. Television stations and newspapers emphasized raucous demonstrations—and ignored the undisputed fact that police clubbed protesters with their nightsticks. These potent juxtapositions of philosophy and political action, disinformation and deliberate omissions, steered Kienitz to photojournalism.

He never enrolled in a photography class, but photo reportage provided a compass to navigate the intersections between the theory of academia and the events unfolding in the material world.

Kienitz's photographs are radical, urgent, insistent, demanding, and clear. The images and their subjects address us directly, irrefutably, insistently. The people in these photographs look at Kienitz as he takes the picture. They collaborate with him in the process: they assent to be photographed. They look out, refusing to be objectified, pitied, romanticized. The careful compositions repudiate the adrenaline rushes of chaos. These images insist that elsewhere is here.

Small Arms—Children of Conflict rejects the drama of global struggle, political abstraction, and the horrific, violent spectacle of war. Instead, Kienitz's photographs laser in on individuals, their environs, and the everyday. These images insist we look at the specific and material daily lives of children living in political conflicts driven by adults.

Risky Dislocations

The deliberate probing exemplified in *Small Arms* displaces the lust for action and the desire for frenzied, constant movement so entrenched in the practices of conventional photojournalism. This exhibition replaces these practices—the endless quest for narrative climaxes, the panic of the unexpected, linear time, the big story, the focus on bloody, false finality—with its uncompromising opposite: a layered and often quiet denouement after the action has subsided, a pensive space focused on noncombatants in the environments and landscapes they inhabit.

These images do not ask us to turn inward. Rather, they invite us to consider the significance of the smallest actions, like a child sitting in a chair or young girls in angel costumes cupping pigeons in their hands. These images ask us to enter into the world and be part of it, to move beyond our own places of comfort into the risky territory of interaction, communication, and political engagement.

All of the potent, compelling images in *Small Arms* speak to a larger political and ethical world beyond representation, beyond their immediately discernible content. These photographs invite the viewer to slow down, to pause, to locate oneself within a conflict zone, to think. They remind us to connect beyond difference, to gaze beyond the central subjects of the composition and shift toward the edges of the frame. By looking *into* the images, we as spectators then can move *beyond* the images into the political and ethical questions of war, political conflict, violence, and economic deprivation.

The Little General prompts the viewer into a relationship with the little boy, his chair, his costume. It refutes the distance that surveillance and voyeurism require. It refutes the melodramatic emotions produced by spectacles of violence. *Small Arms—Children of Conflict* inserts the spectator into the risky dislocations of accepted, unexamined consciousness that all powerful and compassionate images command. These images do not snare the climax of the action as much as they recover the spaces of day-to-day life in landscapes and cityscapes ripped open and decomposed by political conflict. Kienitz's photographs argue that poverty trumps war as an even more threatening form of unacceptable violence.

Maps of Omission and Talking with Ghosts

Suspended between the horrors of the undeclared war in Vietnam and the endless morass of war in Iraq, the photographs in *Small Arms* remind us that in this frightening era of worldwide aggressive economic reorganization, war, too, follows the contours of globalization. Violence has multiplied, mutated, spread virally, and dispersed to the places these images take us: Lebanon, Northern Ireland, El Salvador, Nicaragua, Guatemala, Mississippi, Milwaukee, Pakistan. The U.S. government's efforts to destabilize economies, politics, and democratic social struggles lurk beneath all the conflicts registered in these images.

While on assignment in Central America and other regions in the 1980s, Kienitz observed that media corporations provided lavish budgets for meals, hotels, rental vehicles, drivers, and interpreters—a cordon sanitaire against political comprehension. Many international reporters enjoyed this economic privilege. Some holed up in their air-conditioned hotels and recycled information supplied by the U.S. government. They often worked to meet deadlines rather than to understand and explain the complex situations engulfing them. They rarely discussed the conflicts with residents who endured the horrific disruptions and destruction. Photo editors wanted to publish images of brutality. In the editing suites of the commercial broadcasters, Kienitz spotted broadcast technicians and reporters screening pornographic movies during their breaks. News crews and photographers craved "bang bang"—journalistic slang for action-packed spectacles of combat, blood, death, and emotion. This aesthetics of excess constitutes war porn.

During his thirty-five-year career, Kienitz has alternated between commercial media assignments, with their quest for spectacle, and his own analytical, questioning personal photography. When working for hire, Kienitz's editors paid him to produce America-centric and machine-fetishizing images. Yet as he was shooting his assignments for national publication, he decided to dig deeper and uncover a different story, a story that the U.S.-based news magazines and newspapers ignored. He became fascinated by how people not directly engaged in combat coped and adapted to these extreme situations. His editors asserted that images chronicling the plight of the everyday people would not hook national readers in the United States.

Rather than resolution, the images in *Small Arms* summon contradiction. They juxtapose the rubble of bombed cities with the physical exuberance of children, military uniforms with babies and basketball, the dead with the living. The dead who are buried in the fields and the cities do not haunt these photographs as memories. Rather, the subjects of these photographs are talking with their ghosts. The meaning of these images resides in that delicate interval between the living and the dead.

It is in this fleeting interval that an antiwar stance can develop, a position that recognizes that the horror of war is not only the moment of combat but also the effects on what and who remain after the tanks and soldiers depart. Kienitz's photographs marginalize war and its visual excesses. They do not document weaponry, machinery, combatants, military actions, or white male leaders landing on aircraft carriers proclaiming victory. Powerful antiwar art refocuses us on the human rather than the machine, on the particular rather than the heroic, on the contradictory rather than the unified, on absence rather than presence. These images visualize war as artifacts, aftermath in ruined cities and concealed landscapes. Neither foreground nor background, the drama of war is located in an inert past. The children who dwell in the center of these images do not tritely suggest hope for the future—a popular culture trope that reduces them to victims or icons. Rather, they encourage us to consider that those who live amidst war also live and commune with ghosts.

The photographs in *Small Arms—Children of Conflict* convey symmetry and structure over disorder and the melodrama of conflict. The symmetry in Kienitz's work restores balance, suggesting that the act of making a photograph is a collaborative and egalitarian step toward imagining possible futures. The photographs center their subjects. At first, the photographs appear to function as portraits, but then our eyes disengage from the subject and drift to surroundings compositionally equal to or larger than the subject. These images bridge the impossible worlds of war and its dead and the possible world of the living, of justice, and of talking with ghosts.

Landscapes of Trauma

The children in *Small Arms* subsist in a liminal zone between two worlds: while their small bodies anchor them within the landscapes of trauma, their unemotional stares into the world outside the image express an evacuation, a refusal, an exit. It opens an exchange between the two-dimensional image and the spectator. Trauma, here, exceeds words and representation, carves its marks on the body, on the landscape, on the psychic imaginary. It speaks in fragments and exposes itself in shards, holes, rips, tears, and breakages.

Makeshift Morgue (San Salvador, El Salvador, 1982) is an image split in half. The right side is weighted by two tables loaded with bloodied bodies, severed heads, and a dead woman whose painted toenails poke through her open-toed sandals. Boys and men crowd the left side of the image. They gaze at the dead. A young boy in a striped shirt places his hand over his mouth—a gasp of horror, or an attempt to stave off the stench of blood, body parts, and decomposition. On the far left, a slightly older boy in a soiled t-shirt looks out from the scene. He is neither sad nor happy. It is unclear what, in fact, he understands about the death and conflict permeating the scene. One boy looks and the other boy looks away. Kienitz made this image at the height of the death squad activity in El Salvador.

The motif of children looking directly at the photographer and out from a landscape of trauma emerges in other images from El Salvador. In *Break Time* (San Salvador, El Salvador, 1981), a naked boy, his body coated in dust, perches on a rock in front of a makeshift wooden house with a gaping hole in the side. Discarded pieces of wood, paper, rope, plastic, and rags ring the house. The boy sips from a white mug. His eyes peer over the rim at us. The house and the barren ground engulf the boy.

Natural Causes (La Libertad, El Salvador, 1984), on the other hand, figures trauma as a triangle of gazes linking the dead with the living. A coffin, holding an elderly man with a piece of fruit for embalming propped in his mouth, angles across the bottom half of the image. At the top of the frame, two boys gaze into the window of the coffin. Between them, a boy peers out at us, his eyes directed off screen, his brow furrowed. In these images, the starkness of the settings signifies that trauma is not individual, but social, not solitary, but contextual.

Here and There, Outside and Inside

Small Arms is resolutely not about the plight of suffering children during war and destabilizing conflicts. This exhibition jettisons the fantasy of the photograph as an icon for the passive and distant mourning for victims. It discards the idea of children as those delicate beings who must be protected, pitied, enclosed, rarefied, contained. This exhibition documents children enmeshed in and surviving some of the most serious political conflicts of the last three decades; it shows not only how they cope with war, political conflict, and poverty, but also how they escape through play or looking away. The photographs do not idealize children; they do not invite nostalgia for lost innocence.

While these children may not be the agents of conflict, they cannot escape it. They possess agency in subtle yet complicated ways: they haul wood, stand, gesture, fly kites, look on, ramble atop bombed-out buildings, and play in burned-out vehicles. They are rarely photographed with parents or adults; they populate a parallel universe where war is distant, leaving its marks on the land but not on their diminutive bodies.

Yet the persistent specter of conflict, destruction, and poverty pervades these images. The children are inside these wars yet strangely outside of them, a persistent morphing between here and there, inside and outside. Kienitz elected to photograph working-class and impoverished children who survive on the fringes of war, cities, neighborhoods, jungles, streets, community spaces. Children are the most visible, available subjects in these embattled, treacherous zones—adult men are off fighting and killing.

Kienitz journeyed to the interior of these conflicts to portray the plight of the people —mostly poor, subsisting in the aftermath. Underfunded and somewhat haphazardly, he rode public transportation, rented cheap hotel rooms with no electricity, hitchhiked. As a freelance American journalist, he was able to abandon his economic privilege because he was independent of the large corporate news organizations. An outsider, he journeyed inside the countries to find his subjects. He did not subscribe to the policy of embedding: he would spend time with people from all sides of a conflict whenever possible.

Small Arms contends that over there— beyond—is also here, where we live. The images from the United States, *Nazi Youth* (Milwaukee, Wisconsin, 1980) and *Fleamarket Booth* (Tupelo, Mississippi, 1978) demonstrate an insidious violence: the brutality of racist white power ideologies and the Ku Klux Klan who imbricate children into their webs of hate. These images

remind us that hatred and violence are also inside the United States, not solely outside its borders, and ask us to recognize congruencies between the United States and the globe.

Incongruities and Contiguities

At first, the photographs in *Small Arms— Children of Conflict* appear incongruous. Their balanced, wide-angle compositions frame contradictions between broad political struggles and the daily lives of ordinary children. They seem to express a paradox between big events and small incidents. The children are always outside, in public spaces. The interiors of private homes and public institutions like schools, churches, theaters, gyms, and union halls are absent. Parents, teachers, and authority figures rarely accompany these children who wander alone through empty streets and desolate, depopulated landscapes. They intermingle with other children. They confront the camera as an equal. They do not present the clichés of hope and the future. Rather, they signify a present speaking with the past, emerging from it, yet also liberated of its weight.

This mobility of unsupervised children through landscapes of poverty and conflict alerts us to ideas beyond the simple shock of juxtaposition. It develops explanation through connection. Kienitz's photographs show the resilience, determination, and playfulness of children, even in the face of destruction. They also make viewers see the larger political and economic struggles in a new light. For example, the conflict in Northern Ireland is paired with a small toddler ambling down a street in *Belfast Street* (Belfast, Northern Ireland, 1981). The city street and its row houses, with the empty space of a bombed-out vacant lot where an Irish Republican Army bomb factory once stood, loom larger than the boy. A white cat prances on the remains of a doorjamb. The boy saunters in front of the rubble, his solitude larger than the environment.

Two other photographs shot in Northern Ireland also reinforce connections. In *Milltown Cemetery* (Belfast, Northern Ireland, 1981), a seven-year-old boy in a suit jacket, covered with buttons naming dead hunger strikers, leans one elbow on a tombstone inscribed with "Hopkirk, in loving memory of our darling son. Aged 7 years." The image insinuates that children die but also thrive. Age is doubled in this image: the boy who is buried is the same age as the boy leaning on the tombstone. In *Lads of the Murph* (Ballymurphy, Northern Ireland, 1981), five young boys, around ten years old, all smile exuberantly into the camera. Two of the boys poise their fingers in peace signs. Another punches up his fist. A broken window and graffiti fill the background, a rough stucco wall. Here, we are urged to consider how untapped pleasure erupts in the bodies and faces of five boys.

On the Ground, in the Landscape

Small Arms—Children of Conflict could be misinterpreted as a project that mourns lost innocence, a eulogy to children, those most vulnerable in times of crisis and war. However, simply reading these images as portraits of loss would ignore the compositional role of the landscape, which is as significant as the children and sometimes overshadows them.

Traditional portraiture honors the individual and his or her property. It operates on the assumption that personality, uniqueness, and essence can be captured and then elucidated through revealing, precious gestures. It is static and contrived; it monumentalizes, accentuating a solitary character and minimizing social and historical context. Kienitz's photography reverses the components of classical portraiture. He employs wide shots rather than close-ups. His images examine the relationships between landscape and people, rather than divining individuality. His images force the spectator to confront the materiality of dirt, decay, rust. *Scavenger* (Esteli, Nicaragua, 1978), for instance, shows a young boy with ripped pants and a dirty t-shirt, a castle pictured on the front, hauling sheets of rusted scrap metal on his back. Two pairs of scissors dangle from his belt. The scrap metal spreads horizontally across the top of the frame, contrasting with the verticality of the boy hunched over a littered sidewalk.

In *The Search* (Bluefields, Nicaragua, 1984), a young girl in a white sundress holds open the door to a dirt floor shack. A hammock hangs above her. In the foreground, shadows of government soldiers on a house-to-house search for Contras spread through the bottom quarter of the frame, like tree branches or smudges on the image. The shack, the shadows, the door dwarf the girl. In *Push Cart* (Nicaragua, 1984), one boy in sneakers without laces drives a wooden cart piled with firewood while, presumably, the boy behind the cart pushes. The wheels are made of wood. A barren, depopulated landscape of dried bushes and distant mountains

fills half of the background, the road and the boys the other half.

Kienitz's photography circumvents the visual tropes of power and the myth of the individual removed from social and political context. These images jettison essences of individuals and epic dramas of war. Instead, his images are carefully built from traces of war and conflict, children, landscapes and places. They concentrate on their human subjects and then allow us to drift into the deteriorating and degraded environments where these children play. As spectators, we are simultaneously on the ground with the subjects, at their eye level, and in the landscape.

Noncombatants at the Edges of War

Kienitz's photography probes and then discloses the mechanisms children use to cope with trauma. Children and the elderly do not usually engage in fighting; they live on the edges of war, navigating its ragged borders and messy public domains. In the last three decades, the number of noncombatants drawn into political conflict has accelerated at alarming rates, due in part to the increase in asymmetrical warfare and its various infiltrations. With its focus on noncombatants, *Small Arms—Children of Conflict* occupies a strong, insistent antiwar stance because it abandons, rather than glorifies, the epic and the destructive.

The condensed efficiencies of news deadlines dispense with in-depth reportorial work and muckraking: the time needed for intensive research translates into a high price tag. In contrast, Kienitz's limited resources propelled him to capture images no one else had—and no news organizations wanted. The daily life of noncombatants confused and blurred the reductionist message that good triumphs over evil, and the U.S.-government-supported democratic troops fighting corrupt "insurgents." These so-called insurgents were usually indigenous people attempting to improve their economic and political existence. In northern Lebanon, Kienitz hitchhiked or took taxis from one town to the next, but discovered no fighting or incursions—only rumor, speculation, anticipation, worry—and a large hashish-smuggling operation that exported drugs and imported guns. Children worked in the hashish factory and were paid with candy and colorful carbonated drinks. Traveling alone, he was one of the first reporters to realize the existence of followers of the Ayatollah Khomeini (Hezbollah) in the Bekaa Valley of Lebanon in the early 1980s.

Two images from Lebanon situate noncombatants at the edges of the action. In *Playground* (Beirut, Lebanon, 1982), four boys, around six years old, climb on top of a disabled tank burrowed into a large hole in the ground. One boy balances on the cannon, while the others squat on the tank turret. The boys transform the tank from a killing machine into a play structure. In *Aftermath* (Beirut, Lebanon, 1982), a young boy in rubber flip-flops stands in the lower center of the frame, flanked by gutted, overturned cars.

Behind the cars, bombed-out apartment buildings sprout like abstract sculptures. The vast emptiness of the destroyed cityscape contrasts with the boy's isolation.

Kienitz's own experiences in conflict zones

parallel these images. In Nicaragua during the revolution, Kienitz slept in a hut in the jungle, where large rats scurried across the rafters. He also walked all day through the jungle, trying to hook up with Sandinista rebels, whom he later discovered had been ambushed and killed. That evening after dark, he came upon a thatched roof hut over a tortilla oven. A campesino and his wife walked down the hill, illuminating the path with their lanterns. They served him a memorable and delicious meal and asked him what had been happening in the conflict. That morning, they had spotted government troops moving rapidly across their land, trailing Sandinistas. The couple was unaware that a revolution had commenced. Kienitz was moved by the generosity of the impoverished people he photographed, their insistence on reaching out to him, entering into conversation and exchanging information. Often it was the poorest who offered him food.

Impossible and Possible

In most of these exhibition images, at least one subject looks directly out of the photograph; others gaze at something just outside the frame. These gazes demand that we as spectators enter into a collaboration. They do not permit voyeurism—they knit us into the image, insisting we, too, are participants. In *Wood for the Oven* (La Pista, Guatemala, 1988), a young girl in an embroidered shirt carries firewood, the strap of the carrier over her head. She fills the center of the frame and looks directly out of the image; she seems to call out to us to join with her. This direct, unemotional gaze disciplines how we read these photographs. It also indicates the deeply collaborative relationship behind their production.

The fault line of ethics runs underneath virtually all documentary film and photography. What does it mean to produce images of those who are not like ourselves? What are the implications of the power differentials between those with cameras and comfort and their subjects who lack housing, food, or peace? How do imagemakers work through the pressing yet obvious economic differentials that they can leave while their subjects cannot? How do these images circulate and how are they used? Although impossible to answer, these questions dive to the very heart of documentary practice and representation. They present yet another contradiction for Kienitz to investigate. And although these dilemmas are nearly impossible to remedy, inequalities of power and money can, ultimately, only be balanced by radical social and political reorganization. Kienitz's photographs bring the philosophical complexity of these issues out into the open for examination. Taken together, they develop an architecture of gazes that support not only the subjectivities of the children photographed but their refusal to be pitied, marginalized, victimized. His photographic practice proposes joint inquiry that surpasses reportage.

Small Arms unequivocally dismantles the idea of a passive universalism and instead asks us to collaborate. The young girl in *Wood for the Oven* and the young boy with ripped pants in *Shoe Shiner* (Chichicastenango, Guatemala, 1988) do not ask us for our pity: the direct address of their gazes insists on our participation and our collective action. Kienitz's photographs advance that we see what is possible, not what is impossible.

Moving Forward

But it is not sufficient to end in the unmapped territories of conjecture and abstraction. Let us instead move to the material and empirical terrain where we began—a photograph. *Falls Road Bus* (Belfast, Northern Ireland, 1981) condenses and layers the myriad concepts, issues, struggles, and politics infusing Kienitz's photographs. The skeleton of a bombed bus, cluttered with pieces of metal and wires, straddles the bottom half of the frame. The bus functions as a remnant of violence, an artifact from a previous altercation. The disorder of the random pieces of engine, bumpers, and handrails traces the intensity of the bomb, displaying a cartography of trauma.

The bus looks empty. But ghosts waft through its debris. A five-year-old boy squats on the remains of the seat. He grips the metal wires—all that remain of the steering wheel. He drives the bus. And he looks out of the frame at us, grinning, driving out of destruction, out of despair, out of chaos, and into some glorious territory he knows—he just knows—exists, somewhere.

He is resilient: he has crafted something new out of the old, he has transformed the artifact into an imaginary machine that moves beyond the impossible. He is talking with the ghosts, they are his passengers, and with them he is willing the inert to move, the fragmented pieces to cohere, the real to transform into the imaginary. He smiles because he knows elsewhere is here. He smiles because he knows we will gaze at him and then look differently at the landscape he defies. He smiles because he knows in his bones that the photographer is with him, and we are with him—you are with him—driving somewhere else, together. Climbing over the ruins, we place our hands on the wheel—a circle that says all can be whole—a wheel of life, a wheel of the possible.

So now, let us look again at the photographs in *Small Arms*. Let us return changed. Let us return to a more engaged antiwar landscape, where our own political stakes are challenged and disrupted. Let us travel to that place where we move with seriousness but also with joy, with intention but also with defiance, where the rubble of fear dissolves into dust and we move forward, smiling.

Patricia R. Zimmermann is the author of Reel Families: A Social History of Amateur Film *and* States of Emergency: Documentaries, Wars, Democracies, *and coeditor of* Mining the Home Movie: Excavations in Histories and Memories. *She is professor of cinema, photography, and media arts in the Roy H. Park School of Communications at Ithaca College, New York.*

[PHOTOGRAPHS]

Waiting for Dad

Belfast, Northern Ireland

Digital print, 2007 (orig. 1981), 15 x 7.75 in.

I took *Waiting for Dad* in a Catholic neighborhood during the 1981 hunger strike. Irish Republican prisoners were refusing food in their campaign to be designated as political prisoners rather than criminals. Ten prisoners starved to death during the hunger strike, which intensified the political atmosphere in Northern Ireland. Rioting broke out, and the funerals were heavily attended. The strike helped solidify support for Sinn Féin.

This young lad is 10 years old, he's waiting outside Daley's Pub in West Belfast for his father.

Milltown Cemetery

Belfast, Northern Ireland

Digital print, 2007 (orig. 1981), 10 x 15 in.

Seven-year-old Paul McNally (who is the same age as the boy named on the tombstone) is at a Catholic cemetery on the Falls Road attending a commemorative ceremony for Irish Republican Army soldiers who had died. Paul had interesting things to say: he believed World War III was going to start very soon and that the U.S. Army was heading to Ireland to throw the Brits out; he also recalled that when he "was a kid" he painted the colors of the Irish flag—orange, green, and white—on buildings. But he had evolved to throwing petrol bombs, paint bombs, and rocks, and he told us about the advantages of petrol bombs over other street-fighter weaponry.

The event was sponsored by the Felon's Club, a nearby pub with membership limited to men who had been imprisoned by the British for at least a year. The club was started by the father of Gerry Adams. Adams was a member of parliament and a leader of the Sinn Féin political movement. Paul's father and brother were both in prison.

Natural Causes

La Libertad, El Salvador

Digital print, 2007 (orig. 1984), 16 x 9 in.

Children are saying goodbye to this elderly man who died of natural causes. The only embalming technique used was a slice of lime stuck in his mouth. The boy closest to the casket is the man's grandson.

Aftermath

Beirut, Lebanon

Digital print, 2007 (orig. 1982), 9.25 x 15 in.

Aftermath was taken in the rubble of
the Palestinian refugee camp Shatila.
There were two Palestinian refugee camps
in southern Beirut that had been bombed
repeatedly by the Israelis during "Operation
Peace for Galilee" because the PLO was using
southern Lebanon as a base to fire rockets or
launch attacks into Israel.

Barbershop

Bluefields, Nicaragua

Digital print, 2007 (orig. 1984), 10.5 x 16 in.

Bluefields, Nicaragua, is on the Caribbean coast of Nicaragua. The original settlers were probably the Miskito Indians, European pirates, and survivors of African slaveship wrecks. This area is also referred to as the Mosquito Coast. This young boy is getting a haircut in a barbershop; the posters show Ho Chi Minh, Augusto Sandino (the Nicaraguan revolutionary—and namesake of the Sandinista rebels—who was killed in the '30s by Anastasio Somoza), Lenin, and Che Guevara.

There is also a little red fire wagon in the background. When the young children were frightened of the barber's chair they would sit in the pushcart fire wagon for a haircut.

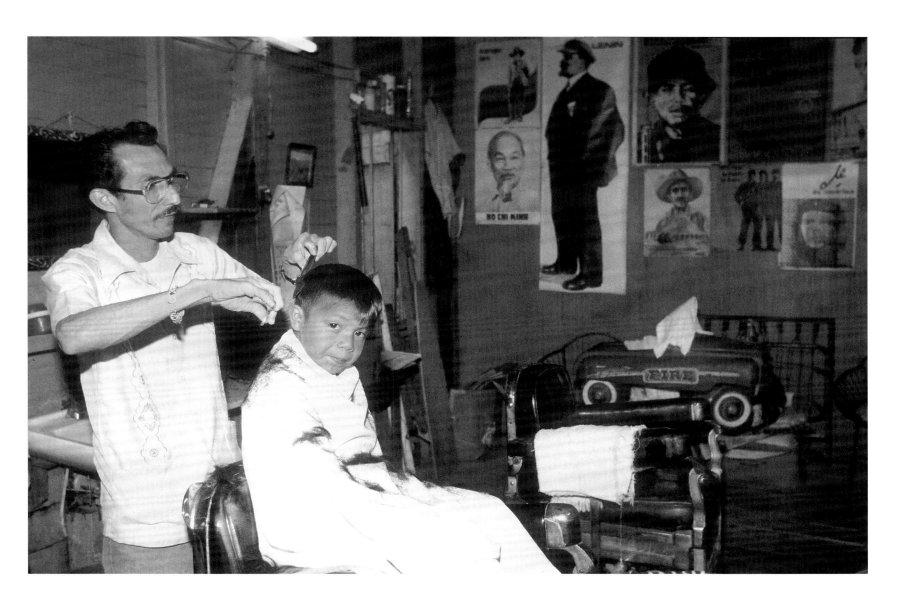

The Shot

El Salvador

Digital print, 2007 (orig. 1984), 15 x 8.5 in.

This treasury police soldier is playing basketball at a school in rural El Salvador. The weapon on his back is a German G-3 automatic rifle, and the children are simply watching him and watching me take pictures of him.

On Duty

Nebaj, Guatemala

Digital print, 2007 (orig. 1988), 15 x 10.75 in.

In 1988 I was covering the presidential elections in Guatemala. This soldier, carrying an Israeli-made Galil assault rifle, is in the town of Nebaj, the last town before what's referred to as the *frontera*, or frontier, where the guerrillas operated freely because it was easy to employ hit-and-run tactics. As a result, there was a large military presence in this town.

We stayed at a *pension*, or dirt-floor boarding house, called the Three Sisters for 50 cents a night. Next door to us was an American artist who screamed all night and we couldn't figure out what was going on. In the morning we learned he had taken LSD and then painted all night in his little *pension* room.

Peace Pigeons

Masaya, Nicaragua

Digital print, 2007 (orig. 1982), 11.25 x 16 in.

This photograph was taken at a huge government-sponsored peace rally. These children had seen nothing but war—first the Sandinista revolution to overthrow Somoza and then the Contras trying to overthrow the Sandinistas—and there was an economic boycott. Food shortages were common. These identical twins didn't have doves to release at the end of the peace rally so they're holding pigeons.

Glove and Gun

Esteli, Nicaragua

Digital print, 2007 (orig. 1984), 15 x 11 in.

I had been in Esteli in 1979 when the Sandinistas held the town against the Somoza government. At that time it was rubble, and there were so many bodies that they were squirted with gasoline and burned in the street to prevent the spread of disease. I wanted to see what it was like a few years later. The city had been beautifully restored.

One boy, about age 9, is on his way to play baseball. The other boy, about age 12, was conscripted by the Sandinistas and is patrolling the town because the adults had been sent to the Honduras border to fight the Contras.

Makeshift Morgue

San Salvador, El Salvador

Digital print, 2007 (orig. 1982), 15 x 11.5 in.

Makeshift Morgue was taken during the height of death squad activity. The death squads, trained and funded at least in part by the U.S. government, would frequently single out and kill teachers, religious leaders with left-wing leanings, and people out past curfew. They decapitated victims in order to frighten the living and also to make it difficult to identify corpses.

This was a makeshift morgue in the Ferro Carro district of downtown San Salvador, in a building normally used for arranging flowers and doing other maintenance for the cemetery. Bodies were brought there, and relatives—many of them children—would come looking for their parents or a brother or someone who hadn't shown up from the night before.

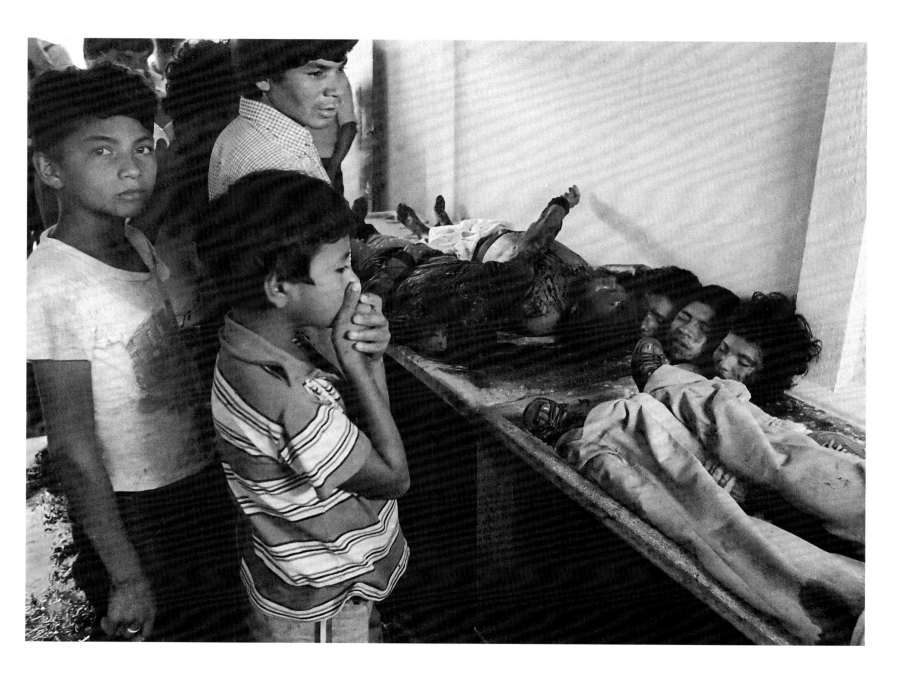

Front Yard Find

Esteli, Nicaragua

Digital print, 2007 (orig. 1978), 16 x 10.25 in.

Esteli was one of seven cities taken over by the Sandinista rebels when they were struggling against Anastasio Somoza. Somoza had become so desperate that he started bombing his own villages and cities. When I came into town this little boy indicated that he wanted me to see something, and when we arrived in his front yard he showed me this giant shell. It's probably a diffused (but possibly undetonated) 122 mm or 130 mm shell.

PLO Recruit

Tripoli, Lebanon

Digital print, 2007 (orig. 1983), 11 x 15 in.

When I took this picture Yasser Arafat was under siege in Tripoli, where Syrian-backed rebels were trying to remove him as leader of Fatah. Despite the siege, he successfully negotiated a trade of six Israeli soldiers for 4,800 Palestinian fighters. The Israeli soldiers were on a ship in the Tripoli harbor that was nearly sunk by the shelling.

Arafat held a press conference with international media. Oriana Fallaci slapped me because I had asked her to move; as a reporter she didn't need to get as close to Arafat as the photographers and film crews. Arafat stated that the PLO, despite this factional split in Tripoli, was doing very well. He said that the dedication to the Palestinian movement could be seen in the hearts and eyes of the children of Palestine.

When I went outside, the first child I saw was this boy holding an AK-47. An adult PLO fighter told me the boy was admired for his cunning and speed, and he was so small he could get into places for sniping and other activities that the grown men couldn't go. Tripoli was in ruins, without water and electricity for several days. He's standing in front of a pile of trash.

Generally the fighting would last five or six days, and then the falafel stands would be wheeled out. Everybody would restock, and then the fighting would start a day or two later, again for five or six days, because that kind of street fighting isn't sustainable. There is obvious fatigue, and so a ceasefire would be announced; but everybody knew the cease fire meant both sides were rearming to fight again.

At night the snipers would sit in tall buildings. One evening I was watching with them; to pass the time they twirled their guns and fired tracer bullets to make beautiful patterns in the air.

Rocket-propelled Grenade

Tripoli, Lebanon
Digital print, 2007 (orig. 1983), 15 x 10.5 in.

I was walking through the streets of Tripoli and saw this boy with an AK-47. The boy to his left behind him had an RPG-7, which can devastate tanks and small armored vehicles; he hid his face behind it.

While I was taking this photograph, a battered Mercedes sped up and three armed men jumped out. One had an automatic pistol, which he held to my head. He asked me what I was doing and if I worked for a newspaper. I said, "Newspaper, no, I work for a magazine (I was working for *U.S. News & World Report* at the time).

He said, "Magazine! Magazine! What is magazine?" and waved the gun around my head. His friends, in garbled English, said he was very angry and I should start walking down the street while they tried to calm him so he wouldn't shoot me. So I started walking; a block and a half away the battered Mercedes rolled up again. They all jumped out and I thought, this is it; but instead he said, "Oh, I'm so sorry. I do not understand the word magazine. I thought you were CIA."

Nazi Youth

Milwaukee, Wisconsin

Digital print, 2007 (orig. 1980), 15 x 8 in.

This boy was attending a Nazi rally in Humboldt Park. There were about ten Nazis, and probably two or three times as many members of the press, plus some protesters. Art Jones, a Chicago white supremacist, was speaking from a truck bed with another neo-Nazi standing guard at the podium.

Fleamarket Booth

Tupelo, Mississippi

Digital print, 2007 (orig. 1978), 9.25 x 15 in.

Fleamarket Booth was taken in Tupelo, Mississippi, when I was covering the Hines trial taking place a few hours away in Cullman County, Alabama. Tommy Lee Hines was a young black man with the mental capacity of a six-year-old who had been charged with the rape and murder of a white woman. The circumstances of the crime seemed implausible: he was accused of driving the woman a fair distance, but was mentally incapable of operating a car. The trial sparked protests by people who considered it unjust and racially motivated, and the Ku Klux Klan organized heavily in response. At the booth in this photograph there was an announcement for a rally that evening in Moulton, Alabama, about forty minutes from Cullman.

When I went to Moulton that evening I was struck by how ingrained these rallies were in Southern culture. Several hundred people attended; the state patrol directed the long lines of cars and the women brought fresh baked goods and other homemade items to share.

Beasts of Burden

La Libertad, El Salvador

Digital print, 2007 (orig. 1981), 10.75 x 16 in.

This campesino and his children are repairing their roof; the oxen are hauling a load of tiles. I traveled to this area with a priest by the name of Paul Schindler from Ohio, who had been living with two of the three nuns murdered (along with a church worker) and buried in shallow graves in 1980. The people who lived in this area were deeply ashamed that the nuns were murdered, and they wanted to protect Paul and me wherever we traveled. This family lives in one of the rural cantons where Paul held church service; the nuns would have accompanied him to help with the service, had they been alive.

Break Time

San Salvador, El Salvador

Digital print, 2007 (orig. 1981), 10 x 15 in.

I was in San Salvador covering the presidential elections and at the same time doing a story about the death squads. This boy was drinking a cup of water given to him by his grandmother. He was sitting next to the house where he lived with his extended family. I was taken to the area by a Dutch journalist, who asked me if I wanted to see "the Coca-Cola culture." (Anecdotally, while I was listening to the radio one day, a woman came on and gave a recipe for cooking "Huevos con Coca-Cola"— eggs with Coca-Cola.)

This boy's family earned a living by making large, crude cement castings of Disney characters like Mickey Mouse, Scrooge McDuck, and Goofy. Sometimes the boy would help his father dig in the white sand used for the casting process; his body is coated with it.

Bombmaker's House

Belfast, Northern Ireland

Digital print, 2007 (orig. 1981), 9 x 15 in.

We were in this Catholic neighborhood just off the Falls Road for more than two weeks before we found anyone who was employed. People were essentially living in rat-infested squalor. The boy, four years old, was wandering alone. The ruins behind him were the result of an explosion from an IRA bombmaking operation; three people were killed.

Lads of the Murph

Ballymurphy, Belfast, Northern Ireland
Digital print, 2007 (orig. 1981), 10.5 x 15 in.

There wasn't a lot for children in working-class Belfast neighborhoods to do in 1981. Their daily activities usually consisted of throwing rocks or petrol bombs at the British troops, building barricades in the streets to prevent British troops from driving their trucks through the neighborhood, or building a bonfire to entertain themselves and burn the trash that had been thrown out into the street. These lads had built a bonfire in Ballymurphy, and they're doing IRA cheers.

Cheeky Chaps

Belfast, Northern Ireland

Digital print, 2007 (orig. 1986), 16 x 11 in.

These boys wanted to know which pocket I carried my wallet in. The photograph was taken in West Belfast near an abandoned linen factory. Each of them went by nicknames, from left to right: Waterman, Cue Ball, Milky Bar Kid, Big Nose, Squeek, and Shaggy. Squeek, in white shirt with his dukes up, wasn't sure if his nickname came from his voice or the sound his bike made.

Falls Road Bus

Belfast, Northern Ireland

Digital print, 2007 (orig. 1981), 8.5 x 15 in.

During the 1981 hunger strike, we parked our car in this neighborhood just off the Falls Road, the main road through the Catholic neighborhood of West Belfast. At that time, when you parked a car in Northern Ireland you knocked on the doors closest to the car and informed the residents who you were and why you were there. There were so many car bombings people suspected any strange car might be packed with explosives. After notifying the neighbors, we rounded the corner and there was a bus, still smoldering and blocking the road, that had been fire-bombed the night before. This child from the neighborhood had climbed aboard.

Playground

Beirut, Lebanon

Digital print 2007 (orig., 1982), 9.75 x 15 in.

In 1982 I was in Lebanon covering the U.S.
Marines, who were deployed in the fall as
part of a multinational force to stabilize the
country after "Operation Peace for Galilee."
This photograph was taken in southern Beirut;
the tank was a Russian T-34, World War II
vintage. It was permanently parked due to
damage, and the children turned it into
the neighborhood playground.

Push Cart

Nicaragua

Digital print, 2007 (orig. 1984), 10 x 15 in.

These children are returning from gathering
a load of wood from the *campo*, or countryside.
They're going back to their village, where
the wood will be used by the women to cook
tortillas or other food. On a chilly night it
will be used for heat instead.

Fuera Yanqui

Managua, Nicaragua

Digital print, 2007 (orig. 1983), 10 x 16 in.

I was covering the conflict between the Sandinista government and Contra rebel groups. These children are in the central *mercado*, or marketplace, in downtown Managua. One wears a mask that says "Fuera Yanqui," which means "Yankee go home." The other child, inexplicably, wears a Porky Pig mask. These masks were sold at the *mercado*.

Downtown Managua was still devastated from a severe earthquake in 1972. Some believe that Somoza had pocketed the money given by international relief organizations to rebuild Managua. The Sandinista government had not had the resources to rebuild once they came to power.

Going to the Field

Nicaragua

Digital print, 2007 (orig. 1983), 8 x 15 in.

This boy was working the fields with his oxen in rural Nicaragua. His complexion and hair were lighter than they should have been due to malnutrition, according to doctors who have seen this photograph.

Wood for the Oven

La Pista, Guatemala

Digital print, 2007 (orig. 1988), 9 x 15 in.

This six-year-old girl had recently been displaced, along with her surviving family, into a makeshift village called La Pista. Because of the killings by death squads, the indigenous peoples were moved around the country, so the government could keep them safe but also keep an eye on them. The right-wing government viewed the indigenous people as revolutionaries trying to bring about land reform and other changes in Guatemala. This little girl was walking up a long, steep hill carrying wood to her mother, who would then use it to prepare tortillas and meals for the family.

Scavenger

Esteli, Nicaragua

Digital print, 2007 (orig. 1978), 15 x 10.25 in.

During the Sandinista rebellion, the Somoza government heavily bombed the city of Esteli. It was largely destroyed, with the Sandinistas fighting at night, street to street, behind barricades and sandbags. During the day the fighters would slip away and recharge. This boy found some corrugated metal, which he might have been taking for the roof of wherever he was living. He also had a few other scavenged finds in his belt.

Sandinista Baby

Bluefields, Nicaragua

Digital print, 2007 (orig. 1984), 15 x 9.75 in.

This young soldier was being sent from Bluefields to the Nicaraguan border to protect it from Contras crossing over, and he was saying goodbye to his baby.

The Little General

Peshawar, Pakistan

Digital print, 2007 (orig. 1984), 15 x 9.5 in.

Peshawar, Pakistan, is near the Pakistan-Afghanistan border. In the '80s, the city was filled with exiles from the Soviet-Afghan war, and it served as a base for the Afghani mujahadeen and supporters of the resistance—including the United States and Osama bin Laden. This photograph was taken at Dean's Hotel. The hotel had live cranes walking around in the lobby, and next door was a man who sold bottled propane gas. He told me there were but two things in life: the music and the hashish. This boy was dressed as a Pakistani general.

Toy Grenades

Belize

Digital print, 2007 (orig. 1986), 11.25 x 15 in.

Toy Grenades was taken at a Mardi Gras parade in 1986. I was in Belize working on a book project. This boy was dressed as a soldier and riding on a parade float. Belize is a former British colony (previously known as British Honduras). It has been independent since 1981 and is politically stable.

The Burial

San Raphael del Norte, Nicaragua

Digital print, 2007 (orig. 1984), 10 x 15 in.

I took *The Burial* when traveling from
northern Nicaragua back to Managua.
The local casketmaker was extremely busy in
this small town of San Rafael del Norte; there
were caskets piled and strung along the outside
of his shop. Curious, our group of reporters
got out of our vehicle and went to investigate.
We noticed a church nearby with a funeral in
progress. We arrived just as the dirt was being
thrown on the casket of a Sandinista soldier
killed in the conflict between the U.S.-backed
Contras and the Sandinista government.

The Search

Bluefields, Nicaragua

Digital print, 2007 (orig. 1984), 15 x 12 in.

We flew into this scene on a 1937 Russian biplane. I was traveling with Daniel Ortega, the president of Nicaragua, and Sergio Ramirez, the vice president, while covering the presidential elections. They campaigned by speaking in every town and answering all the residents' questions about new hospitals, road repairs, and fixing other problems resulting from years of conflict. It reminded me of colonial New England townhouse meetings.

In Bluefields, there were rumors that the Contras had come across the Honduran border into the town or the nearby surroundings, and so a house-to-house search was launched. When they came to this shack the only person home was this young girl who opened the door.

Shoe Shiner

Chichicastenango, Guatemala
Digital print, 2007 (orig. 1988), 16 x 10.75 in.

I was in Chichicastenango, Guatemala, covering the presidential elections, and a shoeshine boy was sitting on the steps of the Catholic church, which is in the center of town. The indigenous people there still practice some of their Mayan rituals in the Catholic church. The little boy is waiting outside to shine people's shoes as they go in.

The Trinity

Managua, Nicaragua

Digital print, 2007 (orig. 1984), 15 x 10.5 in.

These two boys and a girl were on the altar of a large Catholic church. The girl had her hands on one boy's hair. The cathedral no longer had a roof, as it was completely destroyed in the 1972 earthquake. I was looking around the outside of this church and happened to peer in to see these three kids playing on the altar, as if it were a makeshift throne. The slingshot was being used to shoot pigeons.

Ulster Freedom Fighters

Belfast, Northern Ireland
Digital print, 2007 (orig., 1981), 15 x 11 in.

These two boys were in the Shankill Road area, which was Protestant (Loyalist). There were political murals painted all over Belfast and other parts of Northern Ireland. The UFF stands for the Ulster Freedom Fighters, a Protestant paramilitary organization that was a wing of the loyalist Ulster Defence Association. According to one story, their leader, Johnny "Mad Dog" Adair, orchestrated the murder of forty-seven Catholics in the Falls Road neighborhood during a two-month period at the height of the Troubles. Below the acronym is a red fist.

According to one famous myth, Ulster had at one time no rightful heir. Because of this it was agreed that a boat race should take place and "whosoever's hand is the first to touch the shore of Ulster, so shall he be made King." One potential King so loved and desired Ulster that, upon seeing that he was losing the race, he cut off his hand and threw it to the shore — thus winning the Kingship.

Above It All

Lake Atitlan, Guatemala

Digital print, 2007 (orig. 1988), 10 x 15 in.

There had recently been a flourish of guerrilla activity in the area around Lake Atitlan and some government soldiers had been killed. I was walking around and climbed to the top of this mountain to see if I might meet up with a rebel band; instead I came upon this tranquil scene of a young boy flying his kite near the lake above Panajachel, Guatemala— also referred to as Gringotenango because so many Americans went there on holidays.

War and Lingerie

BY MICHAEL KIENITZ

A photograph from 1974 of some Hortonville, Wisconsin, vigilantes—one holding a large fish—shows a world a long way from Central American revolutions or the shores of Tripoli, Lebanon, but a photojournalist's first published picture must be taken somewhere. I was covering a teacher's strike and the photograph appeared in my local paper, *The Capital Times*. That year I also had pictures published in *Time*, *Newsweek*, and *Esquire* magazines.

How does a photographer travel so far? With luck, supportive friends, and cameras that still work after being dropped, hit by clubs, and sprayed with tear gas, among other injuries. Being a student at the University of Wisconsin–Madison and studying political philosophy during the Vietnam War had a huge impact on my view of life and our government, as well as my desire to become a photographer. Photography was a way to communicate the madness of conflict and its impact on those who were not directly involved but had the misfortune of living through it. Witnessing and recording antiwar protests and then reading about the events in the local and national press taught me that the only way to truly find out what really transpires is to see it with my own eyes.

I was also doing photography at the time for the college newspaper, *The Daily Cardinal*, and for an underground paper called *Take Over* —truly underground since we operated out of a basement. These two papers gave me an opportunity to photograph all sorts of

events under all sorts of conditions. I also met Jim Mallon and Leon Varjian about this time and did photography for the Pail and Shovel Party. The zany UW student government group hatched the idea of building a portion of the Statue of Liberty, to scale, on frozen Lake Mendota as if it were sinking, and also of placing 2,000 plastic pink flamingos in front of Bascom Hall for the first day of class in 1979. The images produced from those events were recently described to me as two of Madison's most iconic. They appeared worldwide in numerous magazines and newspapers. A couple of years after I took the plastic pink flamingos picture I was asked to accompany Jonathan Maslow to Guatemala for *Geo* magazine to photograph a rare bird called the quetzal. Prior to getting the assignment, *Geo* magazine asked me to send them some samples of my previous bird photography. The only example I sent was of the plastic flamingos. Maslow later turned the article into a book about our adventures in Guatemala entitled *Bird of Life, Bird of Death*.

In the mid-seventies I met Patricia Zimmermann, who wrote the introduction for

Michael Kienitz in Bismuna, on the Honduras-Nicaragua border, 1983.

this publication, and Glenn Silber. Patty and I and about six or seven others helped Glenn create *The War at Home*, a documentary about the history of the Vietnam antiwar movement in Madison, which he directed with Barry Brown. It was nominated for an Academy Award.

After graduating from college I decided to move to New York City to work as a photographer. My first day living in New York, Maggie Steber, an Associated Press photo editor, sent me to a film premiere party reception for Jeanne Moreau at the French Embassy. The picture of Moreau appeared the next day on page one of the *New York Post*.

On a previous trip, I had met and photographed Andy Warhol while he was exiting his "factory." He told me if I ever moved to New York to look him up and he would give

"Lady Liberty" photographed on Lake Mendota at high tide in Madison, Wisconsin, 1979. This model was reconstructed after the first one was burned by university fraternities.

me work. He had just launched the infamous tabloid *Interview*, a dynamic visual publication that ran photographs full page—a photographer's dream come true. When I went to his office, I was surprised by a large stuffed Great Dane dog. Andy placed it there to ward off potential attackers. He examined my work and remarked about how much he liked a picture of Betty Ford I had taken at a presidential convention. Her expression seemed to indicate that she had just seen a mouse. My beat was fashion and parties. My first assignment for Warhol was for Maya, a fashion designer who was having a runway show. I arrived early to prepare and overheard a man giving last-minute instructions in a heavy Italian accent to some of the most beautiful women this Midwesterner had ever seen. "I want you to be sexy, sexy as tigers, tigers stalking their prey in the jungle." Since then, I've used those lines numerous times when doing commercial photography. It helps relax people and lets them feel less self-conscious. Working for Warhol was considered "an honor" so I was never paid for any of those assignments.

I applied for a job as the house photographer at the Waldorf-Astoria, working for a concern out of Las Vegas that photographed events at the hotel. In one week I photographed three U.S. presidents, as well as Betsey Bloomingdale placing her mink stole into a microwave oven.

Jerry Ford was president and had recently been shot at several times. The Secret Service was extremely cautious. My assignment was to get a picture of President Ford entering the Waldorf and shaking hands with the hotel president. Prior to Ford's entrance two large stocky Secret Service agents in dark suits and sunglasses entered and stood no less than three inches in front of me, completely blocking my view of the two greeting each other. I didn't get the picture.

That sort of photography took its toll on my ability to concentrate on the subject. One woman who lived in the hotel needed a photograph for her Christmas card. She appeared adorned in a flowing pink chiffon dress and holding her white toy poodle. When I got the contact sheets back I had inadvertently cropped the woman's head off in all the frames, leaving just the pink chiffon dress and the poodle.

While working at the Waldorf I was asked to do some photography of Peggy Lee, who was at the nadir of her singing career. As usual, I arrived early to observe the rehearsal. While unpacking my camera bag, her agent and boyfriend, a big burly man, approached me and in a very deep and rather gruff voice said, "Peggy don't feel too well tonight—get the hell out of here." At the same time he stuffed a fifty-dollar bill in my hand.

I lived in New York with a spending allowance of seventy-five cents a day. This meant I could either walk to work and buy a hot pretzel or take the subway and not get a hot pretzel. When finally I left New York I was a wiser lad, realizing that I didn't want to do photography that was of no personal importance to me. I moved back to Madison, wondering if I would ever be able to earn a living as a photographer. Echoing in my ear was the sage advice from

Newsweek's picture editor Jim Kenny when I had first arrived in New York: "We've got photographers up the ass here, go back to Wisconsin where we can use you."

Updating my portfolio to look for work, I went to a little shop in Madison called Great Big Pictures. I found them in the phone book and loved their motto: "We blow up everything." Bill Chandler, a large fellow with an English accent, was sitting behind the counter. I no longer had access to a darkroom so I asked him to do some blow-ups of prints for me. That small shop has evolved into one of the largest facilities in the world for producing giant photographs; it now employs nearly 200 people and occupies an 80,000-square-foot building. Bill and his wife Mary have graciously donated their services to produce an 8-foot interior enlargement for my Chazen Museum

exhibition as well as a stunning 28-by-21-foot outdoor sign to be displayed on the exterior of the Chazen Museum of Art.

The same day, over thirty years ago, that I brought in those prints to be enlarged, Bud Radlund, a commercial photographer, called Great Big Pictures. Bud was in the process of opening his own studio and was looking for someone who knew how to make good black-and-white prints. Bill told him about me, and Bud gave me a job printing his photographs; he taught me how to light and shoot subjects in a studio setting. This was a great opportunity for me and I improved as a printer and a photographer. However, most of the work dealt with products rather than people and I grew weary of shooting Parker pens and Oscar Mayer hot dogs.

Perhaps my desire to photograph people

stemmed from my job at the *Wisconsin State Journal* while in college at UW–Madison. I had applied for a job as janitor there but was turned down. A couple of weeks later they called me to work in the newsroom as a copy boy. My duties included the "feeding and watering" of all the teletype machines and the AP wire photo machine, as well as sorting the teletype copy and photographs and delivering them to the departmental editors. Yards and yards of bright yellow paper came spiraling out of the teletypes, and each day over 100 black-and-white photos dropped from the belly of the huge gray wire photo machine that strangely resembled those noisy old ice dispensers at motels. Each day I saw stunning news photographs from all over the world. From these images I learned what makes a memorable photograph. My boss, Joseph Capposela, news editor at the paper, was an avid pool player and would shoot pool for a few hours every day while I minded the store. I was freelancing for *Time* and *Newsweek* and a few other publications, and when an assignment would come up Joe would cover for me. One day I came back with some tornado pictures and Joe looked at them. There were no people in the shots, just devastation. He remarked, "Try to always have a person in the shot; the human element draws the viewer in."

Working as a copy boy allowed me to meet photographers at both *The Capital Times* and the *Wisconsin State Journal*, Madison's two newspapers. The staff photographers and editors were always willing to answer questions

I had concerning my photography. Two local news photographers who demonstrated incredible skill and attention to their craft were Bruce Fritz from *The Capital Times* and L. Roger Turner of the *Wisconsin State Journal*. Roger recently helped me with the print selection for this exhibition along with Mickey Pfleger, another former *Daily Cardinal* shooter who moved to San Francisco and became known for his beautiful sports photography for *Sports Illustrated*. I am grateful to them both for spending hours looking through over a thousand prints in selecting the thirty-six images that comprise this exhibition.

Generally a photographer who wants to pursue photojournalism begins by working for the local paper. In my case, because of a newspaper strike in Madison, I had to look somewhere else. I was unwilling to take another photographer's job for the sake of my own career. I began reading about a group of rebels in Nicaragua who called themselves Sandinistas, led by a man whose nom de guerre was Commandante Zero. It was late 1970s and the rebels were holding seven cities in Nicaragua. I decided to personally witness and document their revolution. I wanted to see a real revolution. Like the antiwar movement of the 1960s and '70s, it had a profound impact on my view of the world and the photography I wanted to practice.

What amazed me most was that in the midst of a bloody revolution life somehow goes on for the noncombatants, the innocent. People shopped for cars while a few blocks away corpses littered the street. I only stayed for about ten days on that first trip, but I was fortunate to meet photographer Susan Meiselas. She had been living there and documenting the revolution. Having gone through seven rental cars, she could no longer rent one. Her photographic reportage was fearless, highly ethical, and extremely powerful.

Returning to Madison, with the newspaper strike over, I approached editors Dave Zweifel and Elliott Maraniss at *The Capital Times* and they decided to run my pictures and the story. I made enough money to pay for my plane ticket. Thus I began doing picture stories for the *Milwaukee Journal Sunday Magazine* and working with a wonderful editor, Beth Slocum. She was one of the best of editors because she had the ability to view the story from many perspectives, and she gave credence to the photographer's input. My work up to this point was exclusive to Central America but with the support of *The Capital Times* and *Milwaukee Journal* I was able to travel further afield.

One of the most difficult times for me was reintegrating into my life in peaceful Madison after the horror of death squad activity in El Salvador. One picture from that trip, *Makeshift Morgue*, is in the exhibition. I had only been back in Madison a day when I was asked by Dick Zillman, who runs a local advertising firm, to photograph women modeling lingerie

The "Cheeky Chaps," photographed together again on Clonard Street in West Belfast, May 2007. At right, the men as lads photographed in 1986.

while walking through lush meadows. The stark contrast of the two assignments was almost too much for me. I kept thinking about how fortunate I was to be able to leave horrific scenes of war at any time and how awful it was for the children who were trapped in all the conflicts I was witnessing around the world.

By this time I had amassed a growing stock photography collection. I contacted Howard Chapnick at Black Star, a prominent New York photo agency, about distributing my work. They sold my photos worldwide and domestically, leading to full-page photos in the Sunday *New York Times Magazine*. Black Star represented a lot of photographers, which meant that my work would sometimes not be distributed as widely as it might with another agency.

About this time, I started doing magazine assignments for *U.S. News & World Report*. The previous photographer in Central America had been killed when he drove over a landmine. John Echave, one of the picture editors at the time, went to Nicaragua to pick up the body. He asked me to always be careful down there so he'd never have to go through that again. John was a great and passionate editor to work with and is now a senior photo editor at *National Geographic* magazine.

One day when I was in Echave's office in Washington, D.C., he mentioned that he had spoken with Marcel Saba, a photographic agent at Picture Group. He told me to call Marcel. It proved to be one of the best affiliations I've ever had with an agency. Every year there was an annual meeting where all "the eyeballs" represented by the agency got together with picture editors from major publications around the world. It was three days of looking at everyone's work and exchanging stories and ideas. It was here that I met Andy Snow. Andy helped with the *Small Arms* project, freely offering ideas, opinions, and technical advice toward the sizing and printing of images for the exhibition.

In 1981, I covered the hunger strike in Northern Ireland with Lee Cullen, a Madison attorney. We produced an award-winning story that ran in the *Milwaukee Journal Sunday*

Michael Kienitz on his way to work at the *Wisconsin State Journal* in Madison, 1974. The signature coonskin hat was made by his mother, Bonnie.

Magazine and *The Boston Herald Sunday Magazine*. Like most conflicts I had witnessed, the children were making the best of a bad situation. In this case, it meant amusing themselves by tossing rocks at British army vehicles and building bonfires and barricades in the street. But unlike other countries, I was able to speak the language fluently and converse about what it was like growing up in the midst of conflict.

I was struck most by the conversation Lee and I had with Paul McNally (see photo on page 94), one of the children photographed in this exhibition, in *Milltown Cemetery*. Paul was just seven years old when he told us about things he did "as a kid." Looking around at the ravaged and burning West Belfast, I understood why he felt that way. In the article under his picture the question was posed, "What will become of him?"

In assembling this exhibition last year I began to wonder what, indeed, had happened to him? What has happened to all of those children who, through no fault of their own, have been victimized by conflict and economic hardship? This will be my next project: to find and retell through photographs and video the course these lives have taken. With the help of Neil Jarman from the Institute for Conflict Research in Belfast and many reporters, particularly Evan Short and Kate Chambre, I have found and accounted for all the children from Northern Ireland photographed in the 1980s. I have visited Northern Ireland twice to chronicle the impact of the conflict on these now-adult lives some twenty years later.

Along with Neil, Evan and Kate, I am grateful to have received support for this project from David Tweedie and Fil Jones in Belfast. I would also like to thank Paul McNally and Daniel McAreavey (he's wearing glasses in the *Cheeky Chaps* photo on page 95) for their support and suggestions.

As you examine these photographs, ponder how these children have been permanently altered by adults unwilling or unable to comprehend the long-term consequences of conflict and racism. Think about the impact our lifestyle has on the way others merely survive.

Reflect on how yet another generation is growing up deprived, exploited, malnourished, and lacking proper medical care in places as diverse as Iraq, Lebanon, Darfur—even the United States.

As a photographer I have tried to once again bring to your attention, in the only way I know how, the way these children were forced to live. I hope that those of you who view these photographs feel compelled to change our world for the better. The children have demonstrated that they have the courage and the will to endure conflict. Let us demonstrate to them our courage and collective will to change the political and economic landscape.

—July 7, 2007

Major Underwriters for *Small Arms—Children of Conflict*

Chazen Museum of Art Council, Great Big Pictures, Bill and Mary Chandler, Isthmus/ TheDailyPage.com, Wisconsin Alumni Research Foundation, Dane County Cultural Affairs Commission with additional funds from Endres Mfg. Company Foundation and the Overture Foundation, Wisconsin Arts Board with funds from the State of Wisconsin, Lee Cullen, Ken Goldberg and Judy Neumann, Dr. Tony D'Alessandro and Alison TenBruggencate, Paul Nichols and Joan E. Jacobson, Dick and Mary Zillman, Dave Tweedie and Fil Jones, Carol S. Pylant, David M. McHenry

Other Contributors

Scott Hassett, Roberta Klein, Patricia Lew and Monty Schmidt, Rosemary Moore, Sarah O'Brien, and Monty Schiro

Special Thanks

Patrick JB Flynn, for design and composition of the printed materials associated with the *Small Arms* publication and exhibition. Carol S. Pylant and Dick Zillman, for writing letters for grant proposals. The Chazen Museum staff: Russell Panczenko, director, who came up with the idea that children should be the theme; Mary Ann Fitzgerald, exhibitions coordinator, for getting me in the door; Susan Day, for editing this publication and going above and beyond the call of duty; Kathy Paul, for fundraising assistance and therapy. Carl Gulbrandsen, for fundraising advice. Earl Madden, for technical guidance and support sprinkled with Irish wit. Eileen Fitzgerald, for technical advice on publishing. Joyce Link and Park Printing, for the beautiful reproduction of this publication. Robin Whyte, for proofreading. Jake MacSiacais, for wide-ranging political discussions. Daniel and Gerard McAreavey, for guidance and support, Flik Flak and Fanny, who sat on my desk and watched this whole process evolve. Colin O'Brien, Nora Cecchini, Dr. George, and Sally Newman, who helped with initial image selection. Ken Goldberg, who found it easier to give money than to raise it. Tom Naunus, sound editor (don't ask). Framing for exhibition by Gary's Art & Frame Shop. Burne Photo Imaging for professional processing, which still looks great after almost 30 years. Dylan Hughes, web site design.